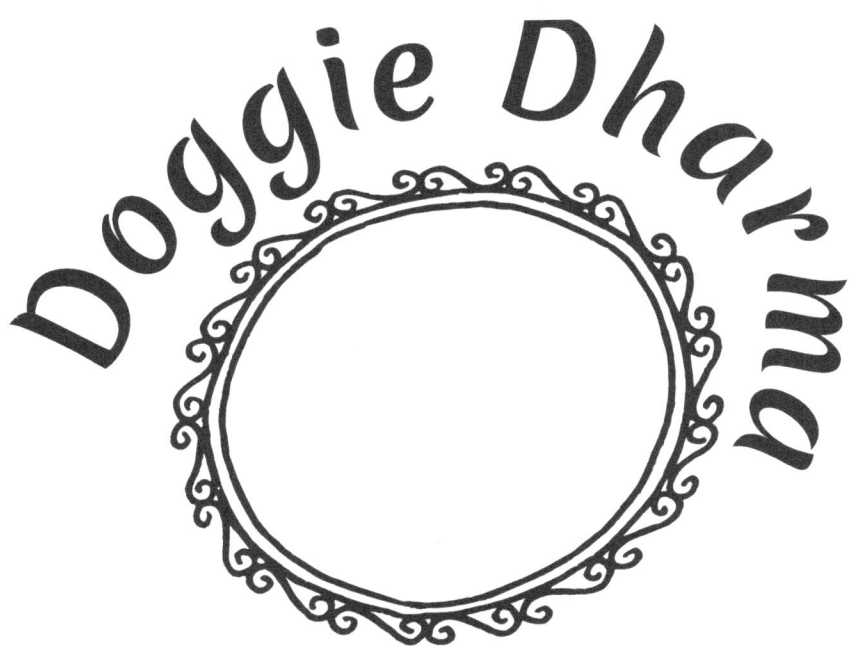

Doggie Dharma

a Path to Practice

ISBN 978-1-7384552-0-1 (Print)

ISBN 978-1-7384552-1-8 (eBook)

Edited by Shirley Lunn

Design by Ainsley Francis

Thank you for supporting the Being Peace Practice Centre by purchasing this book.

To find out more about the project, make a donation or find out how you can get involved, please visit: https://plumvillage.uk/beingpeace/

If you would like to subscribe to our supporters' newsletter, please email: beingpeace@plumvillage.uk

a lotus for you, a Buddha-to-be

How to Enjoy This Book

You will find that our Dharma dogs appear in alphabetical order in the following pages.

At the back, you will find the Dharma Dogs Practice Song, 'Snuffling In, Snuffling Out' and information about the Being Peace Practice Centre Project, including how to get involved and offer your support.

Foreword

Teri West

The idea of an online dog show for our community came to me when I was pondering small-scale events that would bring in a little bit of money, but mainly enable people who couldn't donate the large sums we need to turn Thay's vision for a practice centre in the UK into a reality, to feel that they could do something.

Who would have thought that such an out-there idea for putting the fun into fundraising would be so welcomed, and result in this little book of Dharma teachings from our four-footed sangha friends!

Thor A Rain

For me, dogs have been diligent dharma teachers and fellow practitioners on the path of practice so when Teri suggested a Dharma Dog Show, I was delighted to help make that happen. The process of preparing for the Dharma Dog Show as well as the event itself has shown just how many of us are supported in our practice by our dogs and how they show us profound insights through simply being, being present. It makes sense that our dogs support us not only in our practice by sharing their Dharma lessons, but also in this book, by bringing in donations for establishing the Being Peace Practice Centre in the UK.

Tod Bradbury

Our animals can teach us so much; they bring us joy, happiness, companionship and can recognise when we are feeling down. The Dharma Dog Show, the very first of its kind, celebrated dogs, some of the best dharma teachers we have… all whilst having fun and raising money to help build the Being Peace Centre.

In this book, you can see all the dogs who took part in the Show, their dharma messages, and of course their beautiful faces. We hope that you can learn from them and enjoy reading.

Thank you for helping us build our practice centre.

Bailey

True Playful Friend of the Sangha

I am a 7-year-old golden retriever. I love my human Mom Genevieve and enjoy being with her every day. I love eating, playing, going for long walks, swimming, and rolling in the grass. I especially love smelling everything and cuddling. Life is good.

Enjoy every moment and smell every thing

Billy

True Trusting Friend of the Sangha

I had a tough start. Nicky took me home when I was 18 months old. It was my 5th home so I was dubious. I tested her with every trick I knew. One day she cried and cried, but she didn't give up on me, so I decided to be the magnificent lad I am today. I am almost 12 now and I have my own chariot!

Connect with your loving energy

Bliss

True Agile Friend of the Sangha

I'm really happy in my new home - I've been here since February and have just reached my 8th birthday. I never used to get much love, but now I feel really loved. I get two meals a day, and treats. The best thing ever is the big red armchair I'm allowed to sleep in at night. I enjoy evening cuddles in it and Angie and I sometimes fall asleep together, until late.

Embrace patience, agility and loving kindness

Cookie

True Present Friend of the Sangha

I was rescued from the streets of Oporto and given a loving home in the countryside with my carer, Anne. I'm a Jack Russell cross and I'm 7 years old. I love the sea, eating and being mindful, and I frequently remind Anne to do the same!

Stop and truly love

Crumble

True Compassionate Friend of the Sangha

Since a pup, I have lived joyfully and wholeheartedly. I practice equanimity: loving all beings by practising full-body hugging meditation at each greeting. Sometimes this touches narrow, dualistic thinking in the other party but I know by continuing to practise I help them to overcome this. I also celebrate the nobility of suffering by mud-wallowing in the historical dimension.

Don't run from suffering

Darwin

True Diligent Friend of the Sangha

Hi, my name is Darwin. I'm 12 and a half years old. I've been on retreat at Being Peace Cottage, and have mastered bell practice and shedding hair on meditation cushions. A herder by nature, with Jack Russell Corgi ancestors, if Jo needs rounding up for practice then I'm there to facilitate.

With diligent practice, you can overcome all obstacles

19

Denny

True Inspirational Friend of the Sangha

I'm Denny. I was abandoned on a road in Ireland in 2013. A few weeks later, I came to live with Thor the human. I was skinny and fearful, but with Thor's help, I gained weight and confidence. I joined their clinic team, offering dharma lessons from my own life and practice in the clinic's newsletter. A message from Thor - Denny died in May 2023. Just as a cloud never dies, so a dog never dies. Her continuation is present in every step, tail wag, sniff and cuddle.

There's always hope

Dio

True Fully Present Friend of the Sangha

I'm Dio and I'm a golden retriever. At 11 weeks old I found my forever family and covered them in kisses! We went for lovely walks in the fields. One day I was playing with some rope and swallowed it. I had to have an operation but was fine. When I was three we moved to the seaside. I loved running in the waves. Now I'm 12 I have arthritis. I have fun playing at home. I like walking slowly now.

Live in the moment and be yourself

23

Dolly

True Loving Friend of the Sangha

I'm Dolly, a poodle cross aged ten. I like being the happy dog I am and to offer that happiness to everyone I meet. By making a fuss of them, I help people see how special they are. Dogs like me because I'm gentle and playful. I help my person to be happy, to relax deeply and to open her heart.

Open your heart and be happy

Frieda

True Welcoming
Friend of the Sangha

I'm a seven year old black pug who loves to lie in the sun in the garden, loves to cuddle and play, loves to be stroked and pampered the most, but I don't like rain. I follow my parents at every step. I just want to be part of their lives.

Be open, friendly and compassionate to every living being

Harry

True Mischievous Friend of the Sangha

I am Harry the greyhound, and I'm three and a half years old. I won a couple of races but retired this February to move in with Helene and Dave, helped out by Gustaf and Ainsley. I love to sleep in awkward positions, run on the beach, watch the kitchen intently for food, and am rediscovering my sense of play and mischievousness!

Be playful and enjoy life

Jackie

True Grateful Friend of the Sangha

I was rescued from the streets almost 10 years ago. I don't remember much about my first caretakers although Mary & Pam tried to find them. Then, I went to a house with two cats and two humans (Judy & Bo). One kitty ran far away and the other, PB (PowerBall) put his paw on the slider glass and I licked it from my side. The humans were astounded! I had found my forever home. PB and I would play and catch geckos for each other. Bingo (PB's sister) would wait until we were under the coffee table and would dump the magazines on us and the floor.

Be a friend to everyone

Max

True Patient Friend of the Sangha

My first human family lived in a flat in Battersea. I had no essential dog training - car travel, toilet details, etc, although I was much loved. Then my Elder rescued me, taking me to live in paradise. I have learned to trust cars, taken train journeys, see the others in my first human family regularly and take my professional career as companion and playmate to my Elder very seriously.

Take time to do nothing but contemplate the sunshine and the shadows

Merlin

True Inspiring Friend of the Sangha

I grew up meditating with my Mom since I was a wee puppy, and I just LOVE the time on the cushion! As soon as my mom even utters the word "meditate" I run to the meditation nook and wait for the command from her to jump up on the cushion. I often want our time sitting to be longer... but I'm always happy to give mom a hug after the bell rings!

Just go sit and relax

MikoTico

True Gentle Friend of the Sangha

MT bow-wowing in from Switzerland. My siblings were drowned, but I was rescued and placed in troubled hands with several owners. My family found me very sick and barely surviving. They ignored advice to put me to sleep and we now focus on waking up and transforming my aggression into loving-kindness! We're healing my past, living peacefully in the present moment, walking in nature, playing joyfully in water, chasing balls and cuddling with my multicultural family.

Enjoy interbeing with the elements

Minnie

True Joyous Friend of the Sangha

I am satisfied with the simple things (walks, sniffing) and love all sentient beings, especially mini-beasts. My regular bark is a bell of mindfulness for my human family, reminding them to be in the present moment. I love Mother Earth, especially eating her soil. I make friends wherever I go. I am joyful and super excited to be alive.

Love everyone and everything

Penny

True Generous Friend of the Sangha

I am eight years old and always live in the present moment. I enjoy life immensely and aim to share my happiness with every dog and person I meet. If I get scared or uncertain about anything I look to my friend Sophie to see how I should react. I love running in the fields and swim at every opportunity.

Happiness is greater when it's shared

Penny

True Resilient Friend of the Sangha

I used to live with an old human who loved me and gave me lots of treats, but I didn't get out much. Then I went to the place with all the dogs until my new family finally came to get me! Here the menu is so-so but they give me lots of hugs, and I go for many walks

Be fully present for your food

Pepper

True Helpful Friend of the Sangha

When I was 8 months old, I came from the Mayhew Animal Shelter to live with Marion and Miles. I've been happily at home here for seven years now. I love being outside, especially practising ball work, pass and retrieve, and squirrel hunting. I've yet to catch a squirrel, but one did drop on my head once from a tree in the park. I was so surprised, I froze. Oh well - next time!

If the hill is steep, ask a friend to give a helping pull on the lead

Pepper

True Wonderful Friend of the Sangha

I was born in Ireland and then migrated to Sussex, so consider myself a canine of the world. I don't like skateboards or thunder so I might shout a bit, or hide under the bed. I love frisbee, but at 12 years old now I can't run as much as I used to, but I love walking meditation, so that's fine!

Walk mindfully and smell the air

Pico

True Transcendent Friend of the Sangha

I'm Pico, a 3 year old Chihuahua who has turned Gouri's life upside down! Everyone thinks I'm a cute little thing and I look a bit like Yoda, but I'm embracing my inner wolf. She's entered me into a Dharma dog show and I can't wait to see what she's got to say about me!

Arrive here and let go of narrative and expectation

Podge

True Peaceful Friend of the Sangha

I'm a Romanian street dog and was rescued from a kill pound and brought to the UK. Apparently, I'm a zen dog but I don't know what that means as I don't really do anything! However, I seem to bring peace, calm & joy to other living beings, even those strange folk who don't like dogs!

Stop running and just be

Red

True Open-Hearted Friend of the Sangha

Hi I'm Red, aka 'Mr Meet and Greet'. My favourite activity is going to the beach. I'm a 'Therapy Dog'. People really like having me around. I enjoy saying 'hello' and then I sleep peacefully in the therapy room. Kind, loving and very intelligent, I'm a hypo-allergenic Labradoodle. Sending love (and a big waggy tail) stroke me and I'm happy!

Be kind and open-hearted to everyone

Riley

True Inclusive Friend of the Sangha

My name's Riley. I'm a year old. I live with my number one human, Jules and her friend Rachel who is my second favourite. They both needed me to help them heal the sadness they each carried after their first doggie loves crossed the rainbow bridge within a year of each other. I'm so excited every day to say good morning to them and to see their hearts and spirits lift as I jump for joy into their loving arms.

Present moment, loving moment

Sachiko

True Empathic Friend of the Sangha

I'm a shiba who loves spending time with my family in the park. We often go on walks immersed in the present moment. My favourite toy is the stick because we all play with it together. Through such walks and play, we have all learned the transformative power of unconditional love and presence, and have developed a deep connection with nature.

There is great joy to be found in presence

Snowy

True Courageous Friend of the Sangha

My name is Snowy. I'm a Jack Russell/Pomeranian rescue. I'm soft and tough at the same time. I like hunting but I'm usually a good boy, unless I see a deer, then I'm off like a rocket. My human mum calls me Mammolo ('Bashful' in Italian, one of the seven dwarves), but I tell her not to call me that in front of the mice as I am a hunter!!

Be true to yourself

Sophie

True Supportive Friend of the Sangha

A week after arriving at my new forever home as an eight week old puppy, my owner's husband died unexpectedly, so from an early age I had an important role supporting her. We've been together ten years now and have a special bond of trust. I love our daily walks by the sea or in the countryside (and barking at the postman!).

Mutual trust and deep listening make true Dharma friendship

Tashi

True Affectionate Friend of the Sangha

Hi, I'm Tashi and I live with Larry and Peggy. My mindfulness practice is to follow my nose with playfulness, curiosity and joy. I am very content and happy to be a dog. Thay says that the way we start our day is very important, so every morning I wait to see who wakes up first and I give them kisses, before I wake the other person.

Start the day with love

Taz

True Adventurous Friend of the Sangha

Hi, I'm Taz, full name, Captain Taz Pants. I'm about 7 years old and I'm a chihuahua x terrier. I was once a street dog in Cyprus. Tod adopted me from a shelter in December 2018. Since then, I have become his shadow, accompanying him on mindful walks, sitting with him while he meditates and generally going everywhere with him, including his office. I'm a real character, with my adorable snaggle tooth, affectionate personality and need for belly rubs 24/7.

Live fully in the present moment

Teddy

True Dancing Friend of the Sangha

I'm Ted 'Theodore' Place! I'm a four-year-old Border Collie from the Midlands in a lineage of sheep whisperers, with door-pushing habits and sky-guarding duties, keeping gardens clear of pigeons. By night, I'm a dancing aficionado, grooving to every beat. Daily, I cherish ball chases and toy tales. Yet, I seek the 'Four Paws Mindfulness Trainings' for inner pup-peace and grand outdoor adventures. Aiming to evolve from jumpy to joyous. An eager student awaits. Woofs & wags!

Every moment off the lead outdoors is a moment of joy and happiness, whatever the weather

Tomo

True Attentive Friend of the Sangha

Tomo here, I'm Havanese and my name means friend in Japanese. I enjoy a sniffari (sniffing and safari), taking in the world through my sense of smell. I like to follow my nose, which can be a challenge for my human! Nowhere to go, nothing to do, only to interbe with the collective energy of living things outside our door.

Sniff everything, befriend and embrace everyone

Wally

True Fun-Loving Friend of the Sangha

There was a lot of suffering in the beginning of my life. After my person was caught by police, I entered a kill shelter where I caught distemper and a tick born disease. Kind people took me out of the shelter, nursed me back to health and that's when I found my forever home through the foster program. I have found boundless joy now living with 4 other canine siblings and a mom and dad who love me so much.

Feel joy in every moment

Ziva (the Diva)

True Steadfast Friend of the Sangha

Hello, I'm Ziva. My guardians named me after a Mossad agent on TV. They thought that two years living on the streets in Romania would have made me tough as nails. However, in fact, it has left me anxious about lots of things. But I still love life – chasing squirrels, destroying my squeaky toys, and snuggling with my humans.

When difficulties arise, ask a friend to be with you

The Dharma Dog Practice Song

(to the tune of 'Breathing In, Breathing Out')

Snuffling In, Snuffling Out,

Snuffling In, Snuffling Out.

We are mindful as we forage

For what is fresh, and what is not.

And there surely is a reason

To love Everyone,

We are free!

Breathing In, Breathing Out,

Breathing In, Breathing Out.

Aware of others as we're snuffling -

Who's been here, and who's been there.

And we know that what we're finding

Inter-is with everything.

We are free!

Snoring in, Snoring Out

Snoring in, Snoring Out

We are full of lovely dinner

We are happy as can be

We are friends of every tree trunk

We are loved by Mother Earth

We are free!

Milton Keynes UK
Ingram Content Group UK Ltd.
UKHW020936160324
439531UK00008B/112